AMERICAN & EUROPEAN GLASS

FROM THE DAYTON ART INSTITUTE

THE DAYTON ART INSTITUTE

All rights reserved. No portion of this book may be reproduced in any form or by any means without the permission of the copyright holders.

Haines, Reyne
American and European Glass from The Dayton Art Institute / catalogue by Reyne Haines; catalogue entries by Shayna V. McConville.–1st ed.
    p. cm.
Includes bibliographical references and index.
 ISBN 0-937809-23-3
1. Glassware–United States–Catalogs.
2. Glassware–Europe–Catalogs.
3. Glassware–Ohio–Dayton–Catalogs.
4. The Dayton Art Institute–Catalogs.
I. Haines, Reyne.
II. The Dayton Art Institute.
III. Title.
 NK5112.M243 2003
 748.2'074'77173–dc21

2002154380

Copyright 2003 The Dayton Art Institute
All rights reserved.

Published in 2003 by The Dayton Art Institute (Dayton, Ohio)

Typeset in Blair Md, Helvetica light

Printed on Utopia One X silk

Printed by PressWorks, Plain City, Ohio

Printed in the United States of America

Catalogue design by Jennifer Perry, The Dayton Art Institute

Color corrections by Total Pre-Press Services

All catalogue photographs by Todd Champlin, Dayton, Ohio
Catalogue 38 photograph by Robert Hock, Dayton, Ohio

Index prepared by Al Austin, West Chester, Pennsylvania

All dimensions are in inches, followed by centimeters (in parentheses)

Cover Illustration: *Vase,* Kolomon Moser for Johann Lötz-Witwe Company, Bohemian, 1902. Blown glass, H. 6 3/4 (17.1), Museum purchase with funds provided by the James F. Dicke Family, 1998.30

TABLE OF CONTENTS

FOREWORD

An interest in the art and craft of glass has been a Dicke family tradition for at least five generations. Like most American families, our interest has been heightened by the ground-breaking work of the great modern glass artists, Harvey Littleton and Dale Chihuly, who redefined the art of glass in a way that has not been done since Louis Comfort Tiffany and René Lalique revolutionized the way we looked at this art form a century ago.

We are living in a golden age for art glass and today the United States has become the center of the field. The art, craft, and history of glass design and manufacture is as interesting and varied as your curiosity allows. I want to offer special thanks to Reyne Haines, whose expertise helped make this catalogue a reality.

Jim Dicke II
Chairman Emeritus
The Dayton Art Institute

INTRODUCTION

We cannot say with certainty when and where glass was invented, but history reveals man's fascination with it through the ages. Archeologists have found glass articles in Egyptian tombs dating back to the 4th millennium BC; urns for the kings to use in the next world as well as glass beads adorning the royal robes. Bowls with gold and enamel decoration dating to the 2nd century AD have been unearthed in Roman catacombs. Just two years after the English settled Jamestown in 1607 they opened the Jamestown Glassworks. Through the ages, glass has played an important role in both the practical and artistic side of civilization, assisting in the daily routine while raising the commonplace to a higher level.

The fascination for glass is nearly universal. We marvel at the artistry that turns something with no intrinsic value into a work of art. Think about it: glass, at its most elemental level, is nothing more than sand, potash and a sprinkling of metal oxides that are melted down and then cooled. Yet somehow, the glass blower imposes his or her structure on this molten rock to create a new substance that captures movement and color and light; that is fragile yet permanent at the same time. A common item such as plate or vase is turned into something that delights our senses and touches our hearts each time we use it.

The twentieth-century and contemporary glass collection at The Dayton Art Institute began to take formation in 1997. To date, the collection encompasses a total of more than fifty pieces. The age of the glass ranges from the mid 1850s to the present.

The Dicke family, long time supporters of The Dayton Art Institute, started acquiring glass objects for their own personal enjoyment in 1996. They started with a collection of contemporary Steuben (American) and glass by René Lalique, a Frenchman, best known for his Art Deco designs. As their personal interest in decorative glass grew, they considered donating a few pieces to the Art Institute. The museum was interested, however, in a more comprehensive assortment of artists' work on permanent display. In turn, they approached the Dickes with their idea, and this was the beginning of the Eilleen Dicke Gallery of Glass and The Dicke Collection. In 1999, the display premiered and has been a strong attraction for museum visitors.

The collection changes from time to time as new items are added to the display. The Art Institute has also brought major traveling exhibitions of glass such as *FORM FROM FIRE: Glass Sculpture by Dale Chihuly.*

Reyne Haines
Cincinnati, Ohio

American & European Glass from The Dayton Art Institute

The history of glass stretches back in time to the ancient world. This fragile cooled molten substance has been a critical functional and aesthetic material in cultures across the globe and across time. The emergence of a significant glass art tradition in Europe at the end of the nineteenth century and at the dawn of the twentieth century has given inspiration to a resurgence in this important art form during the past four decades; a resurgence that has resulted in a true Renaissance for glass as an art form.

The glass collection of The Dayton Art Institute for many years was limited to those objects typically found in art museums: delicate works from ancient Rome, elegant stemware from eighteenth-century France, England and Russia, impressive and opulent chandeliers from Ireland, and a smattering of eighteenth- and nineteenth-century American glass that ranged from exquisitely brilliant cut glass to pressed glass examples of true Americana. What was missing, though, was a focus on glass as an art form—glass for art's sake.

As is so often the case, good luck is the combination of ambition intersecting with good timing. Such has been true for The Dayton Art Institute. Soon after the reopening of the Art Institute following our extensive renovation and expansion efforts in 1997, we fell into good fortune by having a conversation with our then Board President, Jim Dicke II. His parents, Jim and Eileen Dicke, had long been consumed with a passion for American and European art glass from the turn of the twentieth century. Their collection of works by Tiffany, Lalique, Daum and others has been nurtured with great love and passion. Jim asked the question: what would be our level of interest in expanding upon what his parents have collected to include examples of the American art glass movement of the past half century? This was a concept that excited us, needless to say. Thanks to Jim's great support and enthusiasm, and that of Jim and Eilleen, this idea was quickly translated into a reality. Our then Chief Curator and Assistant Director, Marianne Lorenz, worked with our Senior Curator and Curator of European Art, Dominique Vasseur, the curatorial staff, dealers of art glass, including Riley Hawk Gallery in Columbus, Ohio and Gardner & Barr, Inc. in New York, and our exhibition designer, Elroy Quenroe, to create a new gallery dedicated to art glass from the late nineteenth century to the present.

Since its opening in 1999, the Eilleen Dicke Gallery of Glass has become one of the most popular galleries in the museum. And the collection continues to grow. During the past year two additional works by Dale Chihuly were complemented by other gifts and purchases. Thanks to the generosity and vision of the Dicke family, this catalogue of the collection has resulted. We also owe a special debt of gratitude to Reyne Haines for her leadership and assistance in the nurturing of this catalogue and our glass collection and to our staff, including Jennifer Perry for her wonderful design, Shayna McConville for preparing the catalogue entries and for coordinating this project and Ena Murphy, my Curatorial Assistant. The project was carried out under the supervision of our new Deputy Director for Collections and Public Programs, Michael K. Komanecky. As we march into the future, art glass has a bright and promising future at The Dayton Art Institute built upon a stunning and memorable beginning.

Alexander Lee Nyerges
Director and CEO
The Dayton Art Institute

Venetian Glass

Venetian Glass

Glass production in Venice began as early as the eighth century. Venetian glass became the leading source for fine glass in Europe in the early 1300s and a major source of income for the Republic of Venice. Over the next 200 years the demand for elaborate products virtually disappeared. However, in the mid 1800s a new glass furnace opened its doors on the island of Murano. Fratelli Toso initially produced utilitarian glass but soon exhibited signs of taking glass production in Murano to a new level. In 1862, a newcomer to Murano glass production, Antonio Salviati, displayed mosaic tiles at the London International Exhibition. He also took the opportunity to introduce a new line of glass called Chalcedony. The exhibit was a success, and Salviati opened an office in London, which finally brought Murano glassware beyond the boundaries of Italy.

At the turn of the 1800s we began to see a change in the design of Murano glassware. The Art Nouveau movement had a great influence on the new styles being created. The artisians producing glass had traditionally looked upon styles of glass that had been successful in Venice for centuries. The 1895 Venice Biennale brought art from around the globe to Venice. This forced Venetian and other Italian artists to adopt the changing styles of the era.

Change would come again in the early 1920s. A new glasshouse, founded by Giacomo Cappelin and Paolo Venini of Milan opened, propelling Murano again to the top in the glass field. The Venini & Co. firm focused heavily on modern design and had a strong impact on the glass movement in Murano, which sparked numerous new designs by glass artists and continues to influence those glass manufacturers today.

1

Pair of Incamiciato Vases

ARTISTI BAROVIER FOR SALVIATI & C., ITALIAN (VENICE)
1900-1919. BLOWN GLASS, H. 7 (17)
MUSEUM PURCHASE WITH FUNDS PROVIDED BY THE JAMES F. DICKE FAMILY, 1999.27.1-2

The Salviati factory employed numerous talented glassblowers, led by the Barovier and Seguso families. Giovanni Barovier and his nephews Benvenuto, Giuseppe, and Benedetto together with Antonio Camozzo were master glass blowers for Salviati, but eventually formed an independent workshop called "Artisti Barovier" in 1895. Giuseppe was considered the "wizard of art glass" in Italy and most likely produced these vases.

CANNE LOW BOWL

SOCIETA ANONIMA PER ANZIONI SALVIATI & C., ITALIAN (VENICE)
1866-1870. BLOWN GLASS, H. 2 (5.1)
MUSEUM PURCHASE WITH FUNDS PROVIDED BY THE JAMES F. DICKE FAMILY, 1999.52

3

Fenici Vase

Fratelli Toso, Italian (Venice)
1881-1910. Blown glass, h. 3 1/4 (8.25)
Museum purchase with funds provided by the James F. Dicke Family, 1999.46

Pietro Toso and his six sons founded the firm known as Fratelli Toso in 1854. The firm worked in the same tradition as Salviati, producing *Vecchia Murano*, or replicas of Muranese antique glass. Fratelli Toso began with production of commercial glass. As Salviati & C. was established and gained success, Fratelli Toso began rivaling Salviati's high-end objects, and soon found international acclaim. Despite the competition, Fratelli Toso glass was eventually carried in Salviati's Venice and London shops. In the early twentieth century, Fratelli Toso achieved their most important recognition in glass production with a line of *murrhine* and *mosaic* glass (see also Catalogue 7), and Phoenician-style vases. These were based on the recycled techniques utilized decades previously by the Artisti Barovier.

4

Vetro a Retorti Goblet

The Venice and Murano Glass Company Limited (Salviati & C.), Italian (Venice)
1872-1895. Blown glass, h. 4 1/2 (11.4)
Museum purchase with funds provided by the James F. Dicke Family, 1999.48

Avventurina A Polveri Champagne or Sherbet Goblet

Societa Anonima per Anzioni Salviati & C., Italian (Venice)
1866-1870. Blown glass, h. 4 1/4 (10.8)
Museum purchase with funds provided by the James F. Dicke Family, 1999.49

6

VETRO A RETORTI SMALL TAZZA

SOCIETA ANONIMA PER ANZIONI SALVIATI & C., ITALIAN (VENICE)
1866-1870. BLOWN GLASS, H. 3 5/8 (9.2)
MUSEUM PURCHASE WITH FUNDS PROVIDED BY THE JAMES F. DICKE FAMILY, 1999.50

Both the firms Salviati & C. and Fratelli Toso, as well as lesser-known ones, utilized several glass techniques originally developed by and exclusive to Murano glass production. *Filigree* glass, or the use of threads of glass, generally opaque white, patterned inside translucent glass (see also Catalogue 8), originated in Murano by Venetian brothers Filippe and Bernardo Catani in 1527. The technique of applying these threads, or *fenici*, of opaque glass in a wavy pattern to the body of an object dates even further back to the ancient Egyptians and Phoenicians.

7

MOSAIC GLASS VASE

FRATELLI TOSO, ITALIAN (VENICE)
1900-1914. BLOWN GLASS, H. 6 1/4 (15.9)
MUSEUM PURCHASE WITH FUNDS PROVIDED BY THE JAMES F. DICKE FAMILY, 1999.45

VETRO A FILI GOBLET

THE VENICE AND MURANO GLASS COMPANY LIMITED (SALVIATI & C.), ITALIAN (VENICE)
1872-1895. BLOWN GLASS, H. 4 3/8 (11.1)
MUSEUM PURCHASE WITH FUNDS PROVIDED BY THE JAMES F. DICKE FAMILY, 1999.47

9

RIGADIN RETORTO SMALL GOBLET

SOCIETA ANONIMA PER ANZIONI SALVIATI & C., ITALIAN (VENICE)
1866-1870. BLOWN GLASS, H. 4 3/4 (12.1)
MUSEUM PURCHASE WITH FUNDS PROVIDED BY THE JAMES F. DICKE FAMILY, 1999.51

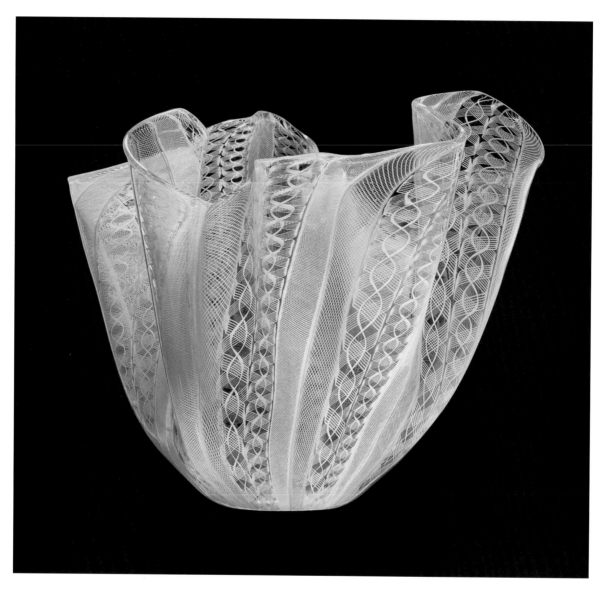

Fazzoletto Vase

FULVIO BIANCONI FOR VENINI & COMPANY, ITALIAN (VENICE)
1948. BLOWN GLASS, H. 10 1/2 (26.7)
MUSEUM PURCHASE WITH FUNDS PROVIDED BY THE JAMES F. DICKE FAMILY, 1998.35

In reaction to the more ornate and complicated forms being produced in Murano glassworks, Paolo Venini, who helped revitalize the art of glassmaking in Italy in the early 1920s, founded Venini & Company. Venini utilized simple shapes and subtle colors. The techniques and shapes, which Venini made available to a large export market, were highly influential on twentieth century glass artists worldwide. Venini often used the traditional Italian technique *vetro a retorti*, or twisted white cane decoration, combined with modern free form vases.

ART NOUVEAU

Art Nouveau

Art Nouveau, a Belgian name meaning "New Art," began in Europe in 1894 and brought about a new sense of design throughout Europe and the United States. Art Nouveau was to bring down the barriers between fine art and applied art. Art was to become a part of everyday life. Common subjects used were flowers, exotic birds and beautiful women. Art Nouveau would be called by several names during its time. *Nieuwe Kunst* in the Netherlands, *Sezessionstil* in Austria, *Stile Liberty* in Italy, *Jugendstil* in Germany and also *Style Guimard* in France.

Organic and free form glass were all the rage. The Americans had Louis Comfort Tiffany leading the Art Nouveau scene with his Favrile glass vases, leaded lamps and stained glass windows. French glass design was led by Emile Gallé. Gallé was best known for his glass, however he was an established painter, jeweler and furniture designer as well.

There were many small firms producing quality glassware during this time. Several were started by artists leaving successful companies to create a name of their own. This explains how one design can look so similar to another, though they are by two different glass houses. Many of the smaller companies did not survive the competitive market and quickly closed their doors.

11

VASE

EMILE GALLÉ, FRENCH (1846-1904)
1900. OVERLAID AND ETCHED MOLDED GLASS, H. 7 1/2 (19.1)
GIFT OF JAMES F. & EILLEEN W. DICKE, 1999.58

Emile Gallé was the son of a glassmaker. His own interest in glass began in the 1860s, when he studied glassmaking techniques in France and abroad. In 1885, he began his first glassworks in Nancy. Gallé was strongly influenced by nature, but also combined stylizations of Japanese art and Symbolist ideas, significant themes in late nineteenth century art. To realize his design visions, Gallé used several techniques including marquetry, martelé, cameo, and enamel. His techniques were inventive and effective in displaying his interest in botany and nature. Gallé and his craftsmen were able to create the effect of a naturalistic composition by removing the upper surface of a lightly tinted glass with acid or wheel methods to reveal a relief, or etching into a glass overlay to give additional depth to a motif.

GEOLOGIA VASE

DAUM FRÉRES (CRISTALLERIES DE NANCY), FRENCH (NANCY)
1905. BLOWN GLASS WITH APPLIED GLASS PASTE SHELLS, H. 12 7/8 (32.8)
GIFT OF THE JAMES F. DICKE FAMILY, 1998.29

Jean Daum founded the Daum Glassworks in Nancy, in 1878. His sons Auguste and Antonin took over the factory, naming it Daum Fréres et Cristalleries de Nancy, and began production of basic glassware. Daum is best known for its cameo and enameled wares of the late 1890s, influenced by the work of Emile Gallé. The Daum company experimented with glass techniques, finding success in the layering of surfaces of different colored glass, creating dimension. In *Geologica Vase*, clear glass was mottled with yellow and red pigments inside the form, and then the lower section was overlaid with vitrified colored powders. The shells and ammonites were applied and carved in the upper half.

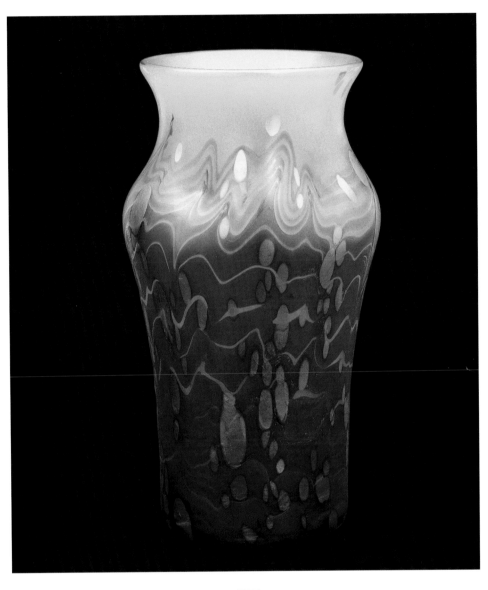

VASE

JOHANN LÖTZ -WITWE COMPANY, BOHEMIAN
1900. BLOWN GLASS, H. 7 1/4 (18.4)
MUSEUM PURCHASE WITH FUNDS PROVIDED BY THE JAMES F. DICKE FAMILY, 1998.42

The premier Bohemian Art Nouveau glasshouse, Lötz Glassworks, was originally established in 1836 by Johann Eisner von Eisenstein. It was acquired by Susanne Lötz-Gerstner in 1851 and renamed Glasfabrik Johann Lötz Witwe (literally meaning the Widow Johann Lötz Glassworks). Today, part of the Czech Republic, Lötz was located in Klostermühle, in the Sušice district in Southwest Bohemia, which belonged to the Austro-Hungarian Empire until 1919. Its location between Prague, Vienna, and Budapest exposed its designers to a variety of influences, including the visual language of Viennese painter Gustav Klimt. Under Lötz-Gerstner's grandson Max Ritter von Spaun, the company developed contemporary styles and techniques of the late nineteenth and early twentieth centuries. Spaun's iridescent glassware (see also Catalogue 14) was an homage to his American Counterpart Tiffany although with different aesthetic approaches.

VASE

KOLOMON MOSER FOR JOHANN LÖTZ -WITWE COMPANY, BOHEMIAN
1902. BLOWN GLASS, H. 6 3/4 (17.1)
MUSEUM PURCHASE WITH FUNDS PROVIDED BY THE JAMES F. DICKE FAMILY, 1998.30

15

LOVING CUP

LOUIS COMFORT TIFFANY, AMERICAN (1848-1933)
1918. FAVRILE GLASS, H. 8 (20.3)
GIFT OF JAMES F. AND EILLEEN W. DICKE, 1999.44

At the end of the nineteenth century, the industry was revolutionized by the significant artist and designer, Louis Comfort Tiffany. Tiffany was the son of the wealthy jewelry entrepreneur, Charles L. Tiffany, founder of Tiffany & Company. He formed his first glassworks, Tiffany Glass Co. in 1885, producing decorative glass windows for his interior design business. During a trip to Paris in 1889, he became intrigued by the work of Emile Gallé. In 1892 he established the Tiffany Glass & Decorating Company, later renamed Tiffany Studios. At the end of the nineteenth century, the public demand for art glass vessels led Tiffany to begin producing Favrile pieces, or glass with an iridescent hue, in addition to his illustrious stained glass and glass lamps.

16

Trumpet Vase

Louis Comfort Tiffany, American (1848-1933)
1918-1928. Favrile blown glass and enameled bronze, H. 17 (43.2)
Gift of James F. and Eileen W. Dicke, 1999.42

VASE

LOUIS COMFORT TIFFANY, AMERICAN (1848-1933)
1918-1928. FAVRILE BLOWN GLASS, H. 12 (30.5)
GIFT OF THE JAMES F. DICKE FAMILY, 1999.43

LAVA VASE

LOUIS COMFORT TIFFANY, AMERICAN (1848-1933)
1908. FAVRILE BLOWN GLASS AND IRIDESCENT GOLD DRIPS, H. 4 3/4 (12.1)
MUSEUM PURCHASE WITH FUNDS PROVIDED BY THE JAMES F. DICKE FAMILY, 1998.34

Tiffany is best known for his Favrile glass: glass with an iridescent hue created by a variety of metallic additives and inspired by the glow of buried ancient glass. "Favrile" was conceived from the Old English word *fabrile*, defined as "hand-wrought." Each piece was unique and hand-blown. Favrile is achieved by a process of mixing colors while the glass is in a molten state. Tiffany explored every conceivable metallic hue, from lustrous gold to pitted bronze. The process complemented Tiffany's sensual forms and designs, enforcing the patterns and shapes of botany, animals, and nature. The experimentations in Favrile glass techniques led to innovative works based on his keen observation of nature, including "the lava series." Lava was achieved by pouring molten glass onto the vessel's rough surface.

19

FLORIFORM VASE

LOUIS COMFORT TIFFANY, AMERICAN (1848-1933)
1928. FAVRILE GLASS, H. 12 1/2 (31.8)
GIFT OF THE ESTATE OF MRS. CATHERINE G. LOY, 1939.178

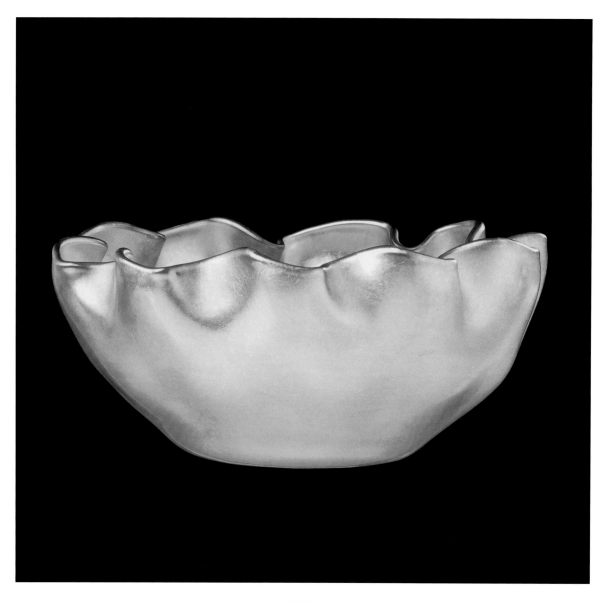

20

BOWL

LOUIS COMFORT TIFFANY, AMERICAN (1848-1933)
C. 1902. FAVRILE GLASS, H. 2 (5.1)
GIFT OF MRS. HARRY L. MUNGER, 1960.33

21

Gourd Vase

Louis Comfort Tiffany, American (1848-1933)
c. 1912. Agate Glass, Iridized Agate Glass, h. 4 1/4 (10.8)
Gift of the James F. Dicke Family, 1999.107

VASE

LOUIS COMFORT TIFFANY, AMERICAN (1848-1933)
1919. FAVRILE GLASS, H. 2 (5.1)
GIFT OF THE JAMES F. DICKE FAMILY, 1999.103

23

DRAGONFLY LAMP

CLARA DRISCOLL FOR TIFFANY STUDIOS
1910. LEADED GLASS AND BRONZE, H. 27 (68.6)
MUSEUM PURCHASE WITH FUNDS PROVIDED BY THE JAMES F. DICKE FAMILY IN HONOR OF DAVID AND LYNN GOLDENBERG, 2001.48

The *Dragonfly Lamp* was a popular product of Tiffany Studios, produced in varied sizes, shapes, and colors. The lamp was designed by Clara Driscoll in 1899, and won a prize at the Paris International Exposition the following year.

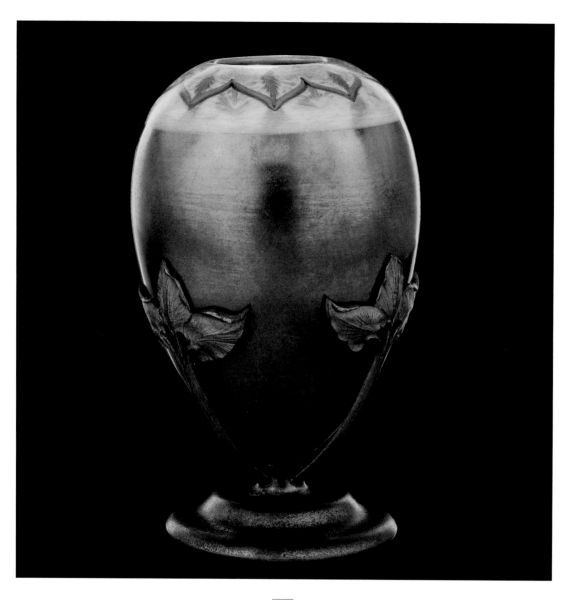

24

Tel El Amarna Egg

Louis Comfort Tiffany, American (1848-1933)
1903-1908. Iridescent glass, H. 7 (19.7)
Museum purchase with deaccession funds and funds provided by the James F. Dicke Family, 2001.69

COMPOTE

LOUIS COMFORT TIFFANY, AMERICAN (1848-1933)
C. 1906–1916. FAVRILE GLASS, H. 6 1/8 (15.5)
GIFT OF MRS. HARRY L. MUNGER, 1960.32

ART DECO

Art Deco

In 1925, the *Exposition Internationale des Arts Décoratifs Industriels et Modernes* was held in Paris. A number of avant-garde artists exhibited sharper geometric styles in their art, something far removed from the curvy lines of the Art Nouveau movement. The bold and lavish colors of the Art Nouveau Era were now considered garish.

The style followed a similar theme to that of Art Nouveau. Again, art would be brought into everyday life. Art historians consider Art Deco a more functional style than Art Nouveau. The coming of the modern machine age was better reflected in the sharp geometric styles designed. Art Deco was also about using modern techniques and materials in art. Originally named Style Moderne or Modernistic, the term "Art Deco" came about in the 1960s by Bevis Hillier, a British art critic and historian.

René Lalique led the Art Deco movement in France with his mold-blown glass creations. Lalique's first passion was jewelry. He began designing in 1881 in Paris. As early as 1902, Lalique was creating glass designs using a lost wax technique. Lalique soon after designed decorative bottles for the perfume company Coty. In 1921, René Lalique opened a larger factory to produce more utilitarian designs. Today the Lalique firm is run by his granddaughter, Marie-Claude.

26

OISEAU DE FEU

RENÉ LALIQUE, FRENCH (1860-1945)
1922-1947. MOLDED GLASS AND BRONZE, H. 17 1/4 (43)
GIFT OF JAMES F. & EILLEEN W. DICKE, 1999.36

René Lalique began his career as one of the most celebrated jewelry designers of French Art Nouveau, commissioned to do work for celebrities such as Sarah Bernhardt. It was in these years that Lalique began experimenting with glass, incorporating it into his jewelry, and creating small molded objects and scent bottles. At age fifty-eight, Lalique had found his second calling: glass design and production. His work of the 1920s and 1930s is characterized by the use of clear, black, or slightly colored molded glass, finished by wheel carving, polishing, and enamel staining. One well-known example of Lalique's work is his *surtout*, or luminary pieces, a combination of molded glass plates with metal bases containing incandescent bulbs. These were perhaps the one example of dysfunctional form and function; however, these were some of the company's highest priced pieces produced. Lalique designed only sixteen *surtout; Oiseau de Feu*, or "Firebird," was inspired by Igor Stranvinsky's "Firebird Suite," which was based on the Russian folktale "Firebird."

27

Rennes Vase

René Lalique, French (1860-1945)
1933-1951. Molded glass, h. 5 (12.7)
Gift of James F. & Eilleen W. Dicke, 1999.38

MADAGASCAR VASE
RENÉ LALIQUE, FRENCH (1860-1945)
1928-1947. MOLDED FROSTED GLASS, H. 4 3/4 (12.1)
GIFT OF JAMES F. AND EILLEEN W. DICKE, 1999.41

DAMIERS VASE

RENÉ LALIQUE, FRENCH (1860-1945)
1935-1947. MOLDED GLASS, H. 9 (22.9)
GIFT OF JAMES F. AND EILLEEN W. DICKE, 1999.35

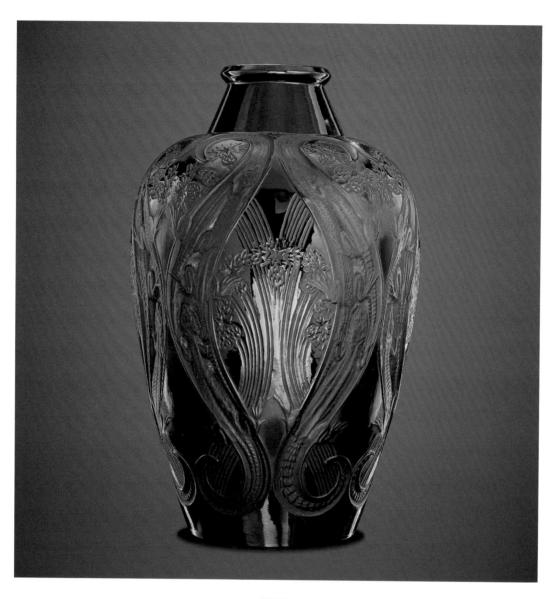

LÉZARDS ET BLEUETS VASE

RENÉ LALIQUE, FRENCH (1860-1945)
1913-1947. MOLDED GLASS, H. 13 1/4 (34)
GIFT OF JAMES F. AND EILLEEN W. DICKE, 1999.39

Between 1920 and 1930, Lalique designed over 200 vases for production. The *Lézards et Bleuets* vase is a rare example of work produced in black glass; it is simply molded and without surface treatment.

31

Senart Vase

René Lalique, French (1860-1945)
1934-1947. Molded glass, h. 8 3/8 (21.3)
Gift of James F. and Eileen W. Dicke, 1999.37

32

SERPENT VASE

RENÉ LALIQUE, FRENCH (1860-1945)
1924-1947. MOLDED GLASS, H. 10 (25.4)
GIFT OF JAMES F. AND EILLEEN W. DICKE, 1999.40

Serpent is considered to be a classic Art Deco creation, and an example of the mature Lalique treatment of a decoration transcending beyond the motif to the vessel's form.

CONTEMPORARY STUDIO
GLASS

CONTEMPORARY STUDIO GLASS

The Contemporary Studio Glass Movement began in the 1960s. It brought the art of glassblowing back to life. For the first time we were seeing art glass designed, blown and finished by an individual artist as opposed to full factories as we had seen in the past. Artists created during their time period as many pieces as glass manufacturers used to produce in a week. Harvey Littleton and Dominick Labino are recognized as the creators of the Contemporary Studio Glass Movement. Littleton, son of a physicist at Corning Glass Works did not start out in glassblowing. He began his career in ceramics and by the 1950s, he was nationally recognized. Littleton left the world of ceramics in 1962 to start a career in glassmaking and together with Dominick Labino, Director of Research for Johns–Manville Glass Fibers Division, developed the technique which revolutionized the medium–taking it out of factory production and into the studio milieu.

One of the most recognized names in contemporary glass today is Dale Chihuly. In 1966 Chihuly studied glassblowing under Harvey Littleton. While studying at the Rhode Island School of Design, Chihuly was awarded a grant for working in glass by the Louis Comfort Tiffany Foundation. In 1968, with a Fullbright Fellowship, Chihuly became the first American glassblower to work at the Venini factory in Murano.

Upon returning to the United States, Chihuly opened the glass program at the Rhode Island School of Design. Some of his best known students are Dan Dailey, William Morris, Michael Scheiner and Toots Zynsky. In 1971, Chihuly opened the Pilchuck Glass School in Seattle, Washington. The Pilchuck School has had a profound impact on glass artisans from around the globe and continues to encourage the art of glass design today.

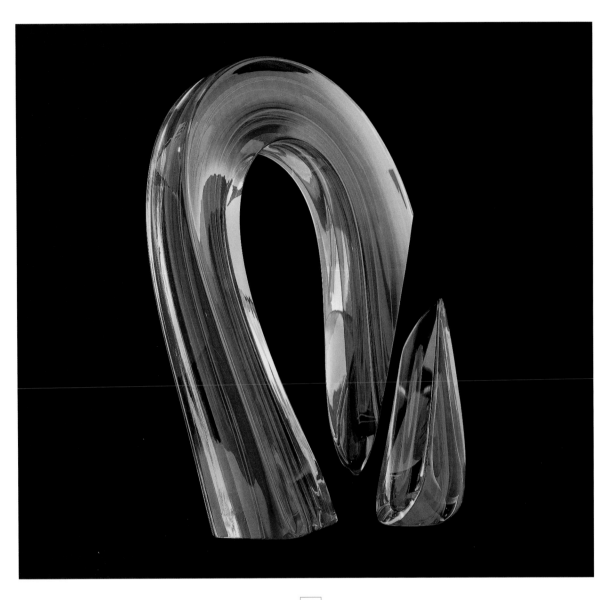

33

Descending Arch

HARVEY LITTLETON, AMERICAN (B. 1922)
1987. BLOWN GLASS, H. 14 (35.6)
MUSEUM PURCHASE WITH FUNDS PROVIDED BY THE JAMES F. DICKE FAMILY, 1999.32

Born in Corning, New York, Harvey Littleton was exposed to glass from an early age, as his father was employed at the Corning Glass Works. Littleton began his career as a ceramist, but changed to glassblowing in the early 1960s. In 1962, the Toledo Museum of Art invited both Littleton and Dominick Labino to participate in two glassmaking seminars. The two built a makeshift furnace behind the museum and held the two workshops with great success. Littleton's art demonstrated a recognition of glass for its own form and qualities as a material, transcending its value solely as a decorative or functional object. The unique and organic shapes which demonstrate the nature of the material are evident in a series of work in which blown glass is incorporated with multiple layers of internal color, which are then stretched and looped into an arch.

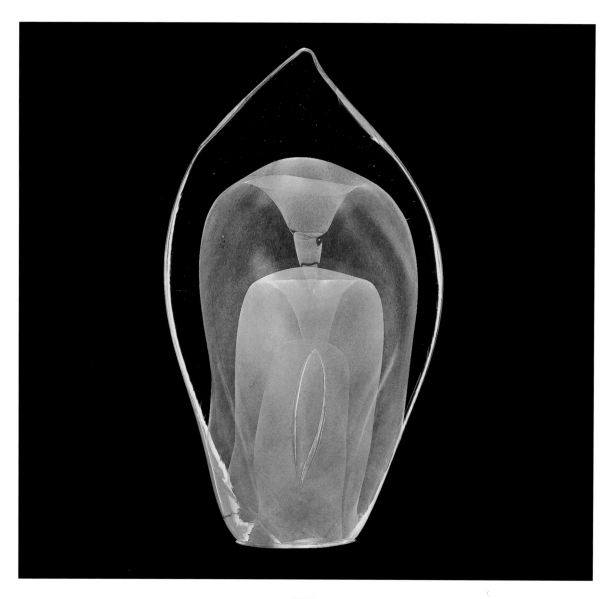

34

Untitled

DOMINICK LABINO, AMERICAN (1910-1987)
C. 1972. BLOWN GLASS, H. 10 3/4 (27.3)
GIFT OF THOMAS C. COLT, JR. IN MEMORY OF VIRGINIA RIKE HASWELL, 1973.9

Dominick Labino was a scientist and engineer, retiring early from an illustrious career to pursue his personal studies in glass. Labino received sixty patents in his lifetime for his formulas on glass, furnace design, and glass-forming devices. The furnace design he and Littleton created for the Toledo Museum of Art seminars evolved into a prototype standard for glass facilities around the country. His advanced scientific work complemented his art, resulting in subtle forms combined with technical refinement. Labino created work solely by use of the furnace, resisting any other techniques and exterior processes. *Untitled* makes use of dichronic veiling, or a coating that causes glass to reflect colors not usually evident under ordinary lighting conditions, and iridescence to establish forms within forms.

35

Navajo Horse Blanket Cylinder

Dale Chihuly, American (b. 1941)
1976. Blown glass, h. 10 1/4 (26)
Museum purchase with funds provided by The James F. Dicke Family, 1998.33

36

OLIVE MACCHIA WITH CADMIUM YELLOW LIP WRAP

DALE CHIHULY, AMERICAN (B. 1941)
1992. BLOWN GLASS AND GOLD LEAF, H. 19 (48.3)
MUSEUM PURCHASE WITH FUNDS PROVIDED BY THE JAMES F. DICKE FAMILY, 1999.2

Dale Chihuly's work has strong roots in his experience in Italy, as well as influences from other cultures, both in traditions and aesthetics. The *Macchia* series was created by means of experimentation and a process of realizing a design through a team of glassblowers. The *Macchia* series, meaning "spotted" in Italian, began in 1981. Determined to use as many as 300 different colors in a single piece, Chihuly found techniques suitable for making his concept possible. The process began with a chart dictating a color for both the interior and exterior of the form, with additional colored pigments added to the exterior form during the blowing process. The piece reflects forms of Italian glass, such as the "handkerchief" vase, and bold colors of Muranese tradition.

37

Metalic Sand Jerusalem Cylinder

Dale Chihuly, American (b. 1941)
1999. Blown glass, h. 9 (22.9)
Gift of dianne komminsk, 2001.86

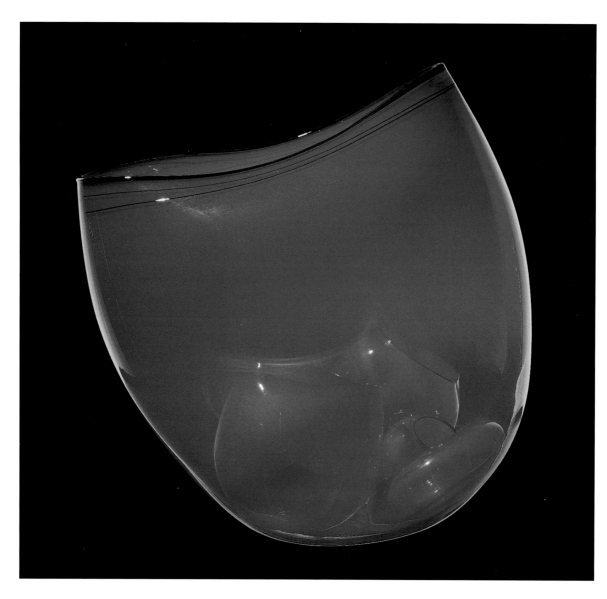

38

Oxide Blue Basket Set with Flint Lip Wrap

Dale Chihuly, American (b. 1941)
2000. Blown glass, h. 18 (45.8)
Museum purchase with funds provided by The 2001 Associate Board Art Ball, 2001.46

39

Aurora Red Ikebana with Bright Yellow Stems

Dale Chihuly, American (b. 1941)
2001. Blown glass, h. 63 (160)
Museum purchase with funds provided by an anonymous donor, John Berry, Sue and Donald Dugan, Warren and Barbara Fryburg, Anne Greene, Bill and Sandy Gunlock, Steve and Sue Libowsky, Elden and June Lindquist, Steve and Lou Mason, Bill and Judy McCormick, Judy and David Montgomery, NCR Corporation, Bob and Linda Nevin, Carol and Richard Pohl, Jr., Violet Sharpe, Frank and June Shively, Doug and Flora Thomsen, Lee and Betsy Whitney, Judy Wyatt, and Bill and Dorothy Yeck, and gift of Mr. and Mrs. T. Hart Fisher in memory of Fredricka Patterson Lewis by exchange, 2001.87

This piece is a part of the "Ikebana" series, started in 1989. Chihuly drew on his travels and studies of Japan and the tradition and art of flower arranging, referencing the *heika* arrangement in this colorful piece.

40

HOPI

LINO TAGLIAPIETRA, ITALIAN (B. 1934)
1998. BLOWN GLASS, H. 11 (28)
MUSEUM PURCHASE WITH FUNDS PROVIDED BY THE JAMES F. DICKE FAMILY, 1999.56

Italian artist Lino Tagliapietra, a master glassblower born and raised in Murano, balances his traditional Italian techniques with a unique formula of design, scale, structure, form and color. Tagliapietra ventured out of Italy to Europe and America in the late 1970s, exposing and building his vocabulary of Venetian techniques. Tagliapietra's residencies at Pilchuck School of Glass, Rhode Island School of Design, and Urban Glass in Brooklyn influenced and altered his work, as well as teaching a new audience glassblowing tradition. His technical skill, dedicated to these traditional Italian techniques, combined with an innate sense of style and grace lend his glass sculptures a unique and modern element of sophistication (see also Catalogue 41).

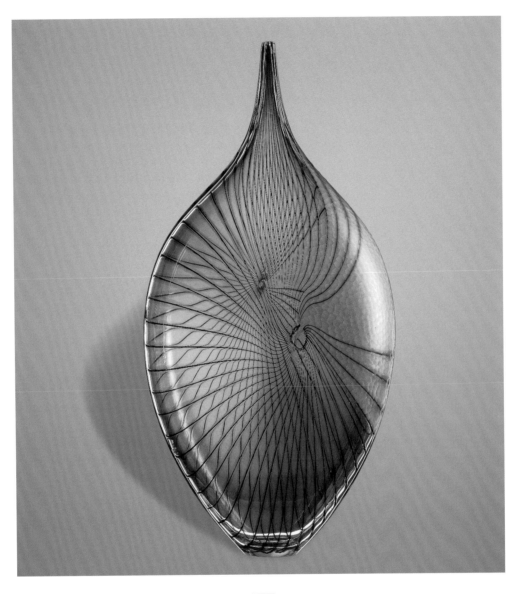

Pair of Grey Vessels with Red Lip Wraps

Dante Marioni, American (b. 1964)
1998. Blown glass, h. 28 1/2 (72.4), h. 15 1/2 (39.4)
Museum purchase with funds provided by the 1999 Associate Board Art Ball, 1999.28.1-.2

Tagliapietra's former Pilchuck student, Dante Marioni, creates art with a concept similar to nineteenth-century Salviati & C. designs. Marioni embraces *Vecchia Murano* forms and techniques and combines this with contemporary aesthetics and large scale. The finished work is essentially a reaction against extravagant surface decoration and techniques, with an emphasis on form, using a limited palette of no more than two colors.

RAVENS

WILLIAM MORRIS, AMERICAN (B. 1957)
1998. BLOWN GLASS, H. 14 (35.6)
MUSEUM PURCHASE WITH FUNDS PROVIDED BY THE JAMES F. DICKE FAMILY, 1998.85.1-.2

William Morris creates figurative work with glass, rendering mystical, mythological, and historical motifs. Morris was trained as a glassblower under the tutelage of Dale Chihuly's glassblowing teams. His series *Ravens* has an almost conservative appearance as sculpted figurines, but on closer inspection, the subject reveals a psychological uncanniness, enhanced by the manipulation of glassblown surfaces to appear like other materials such as stone or wood.

44

Grey Mandrill from the Animal Series

Dan Dailey, American (b. 1947)
1993. Blown glass, h. 16 1/2 (42)
Museum purchase with funds provided by The James F. Dicke Family, 1999.55

Dan Dailey was among the first to graduate from the Rhode Island School of Design's glass program led by Dale Chihuly. In 1972, he studied at the Venini Glass factory in Venice as a designer. Two years later he went to Nancy, France, to work as a designer and artist for Daum Glassworks, combining his learned techniques with original concepts influenced by his experience as an illustrator (see also Catalogue 45). Dailey often infuses his work with humor, using different processes, including cast glass and handblown glass.

ANTIC CIRCUS VASE

Dan Dailey, American (b. 1947)
1996. Blown glass, h. 16 1/2 (39.3)
Museum purchase with funds provided by The James F. Dicke Family, 1999.62

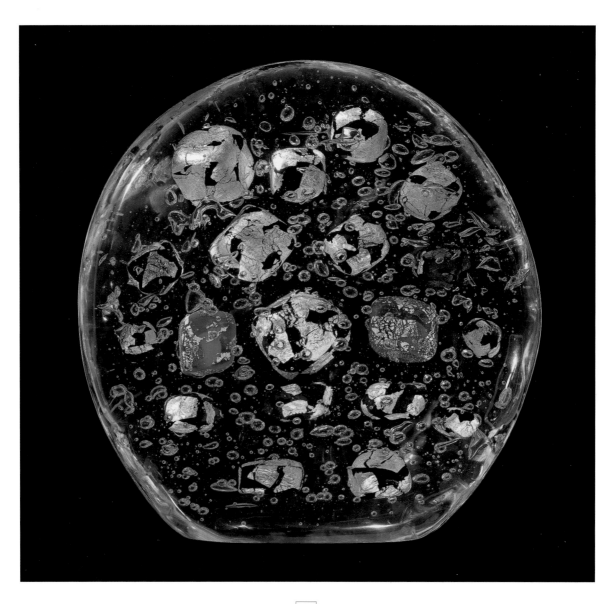

CONGLOMERATE

ROBERT WILLSON, AMERICAN (1917-2000)
1992. CAST GLASS WITH SILVER LEAF, H. 17 1/2 (44.5)
MUSEUM PURCHASE WITH FUNDS PROVIDED BY THE JAMES F. DICKE FAMILY, 1998.92

In the glass of Texas native Robert Willson, the influence of many different cultures is visible in his forms, executed within the traditional techniques of Venetian glass. As a painting student in the 1930s, Willson traveled to Mexico City, fulfilling his desire to visit the country of one of his favorite artists, the muralist José Clement Orozco. There, he befriended Orozco, Rufino Tamayo, and Diego Rivera. Willson's painting later informed his glasswork, where he combined sculpture and painting simultaneously. Beginning in the 1950s, Willson traveled to Venice regularly and worked in the furnaces of Fratelli Toso, gaining a mastery of the material. The facilities offered in the factory allowed him to create his solid glass, free-form sculptures. Willson's interest in Mexican and native cultures are illustrated in the designs and motifs encompassed in traditionally cast glass. The simple and almost "primitive" markings and forms of a bird and silver leaf shapes stand out against the surrounding solid form of glass (see also Catalogue 47).

On the Shore
Robert Willson, American (1917-2000)
1995. Cast glass, h. 14 7/8 (37.8)
Museum purchase with funds provided by the James F. Dicke Family, 1998.93

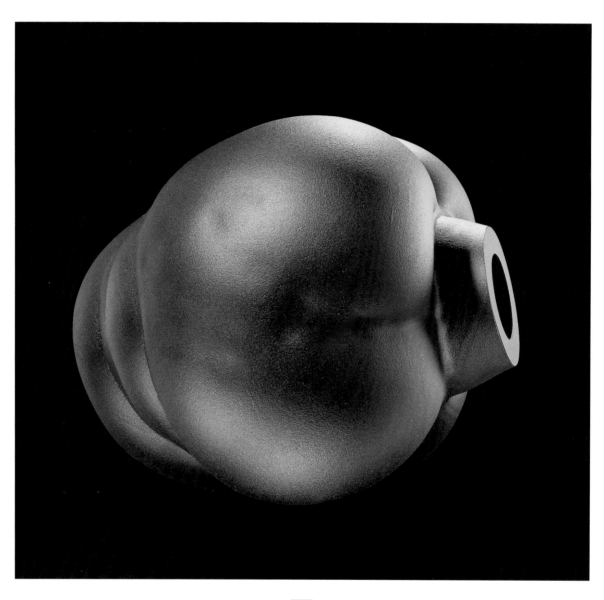

48

ORGAN DONOR
THOMAS CHAPMAN, AMERICAN (B. 1947)
1994. BLOWN GLASS, H. 9 (22.9)
MUSEUM PURCHASE 1999.69

Thomas Chapman is the founder of Dayton, Ohio's first hotglass studio, Shiloh HotGlass, established in 1989. After being exposed to glassblowing as a journalism student at Ohio University, Chapman traveled to Los Angeles and Colorado, apprenticing and collaborating with other glass artists until he returned to Ohio in the early 1980s. He is influenced by the techniques and styles of contemporary artists William Morris, Dante Marioni, and Lino Tagliapietra. In *Organ Donor*, Chapman utilizes the technique of blowing glass into a wire basket. The wire is then removed from the glass, and the surface is etched.

49

BOUQUET WITH BEE AND ROOT PEOPLE
PAUL STANKARD, AMERICAN (B. 1943)
1997. LAMPWORK AND ENCASED GLASS, H. 2 (5.1)
MUSEUM PURCHASE WITH FUNDS PROVIDED BY THE JAMES F. DICKE FAMILY, 1999.33

The tradition of glassblowing is not limited to the influence of Murano. Contemporary artist Paul Stankard creates paperweights made with lampworking techniques, an industry successful in eighteenth-century France. His pieces are technically complicated, requiring a mastery of the skills of lampworking. Flame or lampwork uses very small rods of glass, which are heated section by section over a flame. The heat softens the glass which is shaped and fused to other manipulated glass rods. This technique allows for rich detail and realistic rendering. These techniques were important to the decorative element of paperweights, with the final step of encasing the lampwork in a globe of molten glass. Stankard has found a balance between this meticulous traditional skill and his own artistic concepts. His lampworked glass displays a close examination of nature and botanical specimens, with intricate scenes from his imagination. Stankard's signature "root people" are small figures intertwined in botany studies, often as roots. His mastery is evident in the micro-detail of insects, petals, and leaves.

$\boxed{50}$

Flower Garden

Kyohei Fujita, Japanese (b. 1921)
1998. Mold-blown glass, with gold and platinum foil, and gilt silver fittings, h. 6 (15.3)
Museum purchase with funds provided by the James F. Dicke Family, 1999.30

Kyohei Fujita, one of Japan's most famous glass artists, has produced and exhibited glass internationally for the last quarter-century. In 1977, Fujita traveled to Murano to work with Italian master glassblowers. In *Flower Garden*, the glass casket is part of a series based on traditional Japanese ornamented caskets merged with Heian Period Japanese lacquer storage boxes. This piece demonstrates Fujita's combination of international glass techniques with traditional Italian influences. To fabricate these works Fujita's team blows hot glass into separate molds for the top and bottom. Then Fujita applies gold or silver foil inclusions and encases them once more in blown glass. After cooling, the glass sections are sandblasted and hand-finished. Metal mounts are added as a part of the final assembly.

$\boxed{51}$

KOURIN VASE

KUNIAKI KUROKI, JAPANESE (B. 1945)
1994. BLOWN GLASS WITH GOLD AND PLATINUM LEAF, H. 12 (30.5)
MUSEUM PURCHASE IN HONOR OF JOHN C. LOMBARD, PRESIDENT OF THE DAYTON ART INSTITUTE BOARD OF TRUSTEES,
1994-1997, 1997.24

Kuniaki Kuroki represents the second-generation Japanese art glass school. His work is indebted both to that of Kyohei Fujita and the time honored techniques developed by the Venetians. Kuroki, like Fujita and Robert Willson, uses gold and silver leaf in his process. He then combines it with murrhine techniques to create vessels of unusual richness and allure.

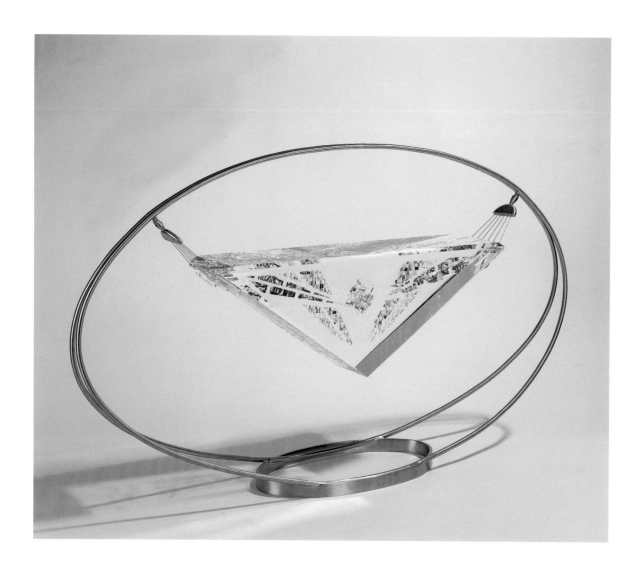

52

BOLD ENDEAVOR

JON KUHN, AMERICAN (B. 1949)
1998. LAMINATED, CUT, AND POLISHED GLASS, H. 9 1/2 (24.1)
MUSEUM PURCHASE WITH FUNDS PROVIDED BY THE JAMES F. DICKE FAMILY, 1999.56

Jon Kuhn manipulates optical sheet glass with industrial grinders to create his mesmerizing sculptures, whose focus becomes the interiors, where intimate reflective colored cubes, created of thinly ground and polished glass strips are layered and stacked together within a larger geometric shape of clear glass panels. Kuhn's intricate patterns reflect his interest in weaving, mathematics and music.

CELEBRATION

CHRISTOPHER RIES, AMERICAN (B. 1952)
1998. CUT AND POLISHED GLASS, H. 17 (43.2)
MUSEUM PURCHASE WITH FUNDS PROVIDED BY THE JAMES F. DICKE FAMILY, 1999.31

Originally from Ohio, Christopher Ries studied with and assisted Harvey Littleton at the University of Wisconsin in the 1970s. Ries began as a glassblower, switching over to sculpting from cold glass soon after leaving school. He works with optical glass, and methods of cutting, grinding, and polishing to create the finished product. Some of his works are the largest unassembled pieces of sculpted crystal. In *Celebration*, Ries uses the finest colorless optical glass, cut and polished into simple shapes. As the work is viewed at various angles, the refraction of light within appears to alter and change the designs on the interior.

54

FLEEING CHAOS

TOOTS ZYNSKY, AMERICAN (B. 1951)
1996. FUSED GLASS THREADS, H. 12 1/2 (31.8)
MUSEUM PURCHASE WITH FUNDS PROVIDED BY THE JAMES F. DICKE FAMILY, 1999.60

Toots Zynsky has found an entirely new expression for glassmaking based on old methods. Zynsky's work is recognizable by her unique, multicolored, gestural glass vessels. Zynsky experimented and developed her technique, named "filet de verre," or netted glass, as an undergraduate student at the Rhode Island School of Design, where she studied under Dale Chihuly. Her process involves fusing parallel layers of colored glass filaments, which are then slumped into basket forms in a kiln. Zynsky's subject matter is influenced by concepts of chaos, illusion, and experience, all in relationship to the material and her process.

$$\boxed{55}$$

HEAD II, HEAD XIII, HEAD VI

BERTIL VALLIEN, SWEDISH (B. 1938)
1998. CAST GLASS, H. 8 1/4 (22)
GIFT OF THE JAMES F. DICKE FAMILY, 1999.124-6

Bertil Vallien is one of Sweden's most celebrated glass artists. His work began in the 1960s, and is based on industrial facilities, making his large-scale works and experiments possible. The heads in the collection are made from casts from two separate molds that are then fused together and finished with different surface treatments. The glass is manipulated to accent the concepts of the subjects, using transparency, opacity, and varying materials to create emotion, mystery, and spirituality.

GLOSSARY OF GLASS TERMS

ACID-ETCHING - THE PROCESS OF CUTTING A DESIGN INTO GLASS USING ACID AS THE CUTTING AGENT. THE PATTERN TO BE ETCHED IS TRANSFERRED FROM AN ETCHING PLATE TO THE SURFACE OF THE GLASS WITH AN ACID RESIST MADE OF BEESWAX. THE VESSEL IS THEN EXPOSED TO HYDROFLUORIC ACID OR ACID FUMES, WHICH ETCH THE UNPROTECTED SURFACE AREAS, THUS LEAVING A FROSTED DESIGN WHEN THE PROTECTIVE LAYER IS REMOVED. SOME COMPANIES USE A METAL PLATE RATHER THAN A RESIST TO PROTECT THE AREAS THAT ARE TO REMAIN UNAFFECTED.

ACID FINISH - A MATTE FINISH ON GLASSWARE THAT IS ACHIEVED BY EXPOSING THE ENTIRE SURFACE OF A PIECE TO ACID FUMES DURING THE FINISHING PROCESS. MORE RARELY, THE FINISH IS OBTAINED BY THE USE OF A MECHANICAL GRINDING WHEEL. (SEE **SATIN**)

AMBERINA - GLASS WITH SHADES FROM RED AT THE TOP TO AMBER NEAR THE BASE. COOLING AND REHEATING THE TOP PORTION OF THE GLASS CREATE THE SHADINGS IN THE FINISHED PRODUCT.

ANNEALING - THE GRADUAL COOLING OF HOT GLASS TO PREVENT STRESS FRACTURES AND BREAKAGE. THE GLASS MOVES ON A CONVEYER BELT THROUGH A HOT CHAMBER, OR ANNEALING OVEN, FOLLOWED BY A LONG TUNNEL IN WHICH COOLING OCCURS. THE ANNEALING PROCESS TAKES ANYWHERE FROM TEN MINUTES TO THREE WEEKS DEPENDING ON THE TYPE OF ARTICLE.

APPLIED - A SEPARATE PIECE OF MOLTEN GLASS ATTACHED BY HAND TO A GLASS VESSEL, TYPICALLY A HANDLE. MOST OFTEN USED WITH FREE-BLOWN OR MOLD-BLOWN PIECES BUT ALSO USED WITH EARLY PRESSED GLASS.

APPLIQUÉD GLASS - A TYPE OF DECORATIVE GLASS THAT FEATURES HAND-APPLIED THREE-DIMENSIONAL GLASS TRIM, OFTEN IN THE FORM OF FRUIT OR FLOWERING VINES. THIS TRIM IS APPLIED IN THE SEMI-MOLTEN STATE WHILE THE MAIN OBJECT IS STILL EXTREMELY HOT SO THAT THE APPLIQUÉ BECOMES AN INTEGRAL PART OF THE PIECE.

AVVENTURINA OR AVENTURINE - A DECORATIVE PROCESS WHERE SMALL, SPARKLING PARTICLES OF METAL ARE SUSPENDED BETWEEN A CLEAR OUTER LAYER AND COLORED INNER CASING OF GLASS TO FORM A PATTERN.

BATCH - The mixture of chemicals that are melted to make glass. Silica, potash, and soda ash are the primary ingredients of glass.

BLOWING - The technique of blowing through a blowpipe or blowing iron into molten glass to produce glass vessels.

CAMEO GLASS - Glass that is composed of two or more layers of glass, most often of contrasting colors, which are then carved through the surface with decorative designs. The English revived this ancient Roman technique in the late nineteenth century and English examples usually feature a white outer surface cut through to expose a single color background. English cameo often features classical and botanical designs whereas the slightly later French cameo often features more abstract naturalistic and landscape designs in more than two colors. Cameo carving can be done either by hand or with the use of acid.

CANE - The glass rod used in striped glass and twisted filigree. Canes are also sliced so that sections of polychrome patterns can be used in **MOSAIC** or **MURRHINE GLASS**.

CASED GLASS - The use of two layers of contrasting glass that are fused together to create one piece. The inner layer may be blown into the outer layer while the formed glass is still hot, or the piece in one color may be dipped into the molten glass of another color while it is hot. **CAMEO GLASS** is a form of cased glass.

CAST FIGURE MOLD - A type of glass mold that is cast directly from a sculpted model, resulting in the transfer of very fine details to the mold without the need for additional milling. Reuben Haley (American, 1872-1933) is credited with the perfection of this technique.

CHIP MOLD - A type of glass mold where the pattern is cut or "chipped" into the surface of the iron mold with hammer and chisel.

CORE-FORMING - A technique of placing molten glass over a mold, or core, usually made of clay. The glass is fused in a furnace and the mold is removed from the vessel.

CRIMPING - A method of decorating the rims of bowls and vases. While the glass was still hot, the glassworker would manipulate the shape with a special tool, often forming a ruffled or ribbon-like design around the edge.

ENAMELED DECORATION - A form of decoration used on many types of Victorian Art glass. White or colored enamel paints were generally hand-painted on a finished piece of glass, which was then refired to bake on the enamel decoration.

ETCHED MOLD - A type of glass mold where the pattern is etched rather than cut into the surface of the mold using acid. This type of mold produces very fine detail in the pressed pattern on the glass.

ETCHING - Design cut into glass; the two main types are acid etching and needle etching.

FILIGRANA OR FILIGREE - the use of threads of glass, usually white opaque, patterned inside translucent glass. Filigrana is "threadgrained" in Italian.

FIRED ON - Color applied to the surface of an article then baked to fuse the color to the glass permanently. This technique may be used to color an entire piece or to highlight the details.

FIRE-POLISHING - A process used to finish mold-blown and pressed glass where a piece is reheated just enough to smooth out the mold seams without distorting the overall pattern.

FLASHED ON - The use of a transparent colored stain to highlight an item of crystal glass. After the stain, usually ruby or amber in color is applied, the item is reheated to fuse the stain to the surface of the glass. Flashing tends to wear off, while fired on color does not wear off with use.

GATHER - A ball of molten glass that the glassblower "gathers" on the end of a blowpipe or punty rod.

HANDKERCHIEF VASE - A form of vase most often seen in twentieth-century Venetian glass where the sides of the piece are pulled straight up and randomly pleated to resemble a large handkerchief.

Hot Metal Man - Person who formulates and supervises the mixing of batches in a glass factory. Also called the "batch man" or "color man," he is the person responsible for creating the formulas for the different colored glass each company produced. As these recipes were highly guarded secrets, a good hot metal man is often critical to the success of the glass company.

Iridescence - A shiny, rainbow-like finish on the surface of a piece of glass. Spraying metallic salts on the still hot glass and refiring the piece achieves the effect. Different effects are achieved by varying the color of the underlying glass and the combination of metallic elements.

Jack-in-the-Pulpit Vase - A form of vase with the rim manipulated to resemble the wildflower of the same name. Generally, the back edge is curled up while the front edge is curled downward. This form was most famously used by Louis Comfort Tiffany.

Knob or Knop - A finial on a lid or a bulbous section on the stem of a goblet or wineglass.

Lampwork - Referring to forming delicate objects out of thin rods or canes of glass while working at the lamp, small torch, or a small flame.

Latticino - An Italian term for the art of embedding spiral threads of white or colored glass in clear crystal. The technique dates back to glassmaking in the Roman Empire and is the most distinctive technique used in Murano glass today.

Lattimo - The opaque white glass, or milk glass, that resembles porcelain when used to case or form a vessel. It is also used in various bold techniques.

Millefiori - An Italian term meaning "thousand flowers," this glass was also called "tessera" or tile work. Glass rods are cut into discs, placed into a mold in a particular pattern and then refired until fused. The technique is found on plates, vases, and bowls and in the interior of paperweights.

Mold/Mould - Encasement into which hot glass is poured or blown to form an object. A pattern is made in wood or plaster that is sent to the metal foundry where a rough iron cast is made. The mold is then milled, shaped and finally the design is cut or etched into the surface. (**See Chip Mold, Etched Mold,** and **Cast Figure Mold**)

Mold-Blown - A method of glass production where a gather of molten glass is blown into a patterned mold to produce an object such as a bottle or vase.

Mold-Pressed or **Press Molded -** A method of glass production where molten glass is poured into a mold and a plunger is brought down which presses glass into all parts of the mold.

Mosaic glass or Millefiori - Done in the same technique as **Murrhine Glass**, with a soft layer of skin of clear glass placed on to the murrhine and fused, creating a clear glass interior with murrhine as the outside decoration.

Murrhine - Disks of colored glass, often with colorful and complicated patterns.

Murrhine Glass - Glassware made with fused pieces of **Murrhine** that are then shaped into the desired form, and after cooled, the form is polished to reveal the patterns of the murrhine.

Nappy - Another word for a bowl.

Novelty - A pressed glass object generally made in the form of some larger item like a hatchet, boat or animal. They were extremely popular in the late nineteenth century with many produced as match holders, toothpick holders and small dresser boxes.

Opal - This was the term used in the nineteenth century to describe the solid white glass today known as milk glass.

Opalescent - Semi-translucent, milky white glass that shows orange (or fire) when held to a strong light. Opalescent glass is often found around the edge of a piece, flowing into another color glass.

Ormolu - Decorative gilded bronze adornments added to a glass item.

Overshot - Type of glass produced by rolling the **Gather** over a steel plate covered with minute glass particles. The gather is reheated to melt the sharp edges of the fragments and then blown to the finished size. The resulting item has contrasting color specks and a slightly rough surface texture. In rare examples, the gather is first blown to shape and then rolled in the fragments without being refired. The surface on such pieces is quite uneven and sharp to the touch.

PIE DOUCHE - French term referring to a paperweight that is raised on a low, pedestal foot.

PONTIL MARK - The scar left on the base of a glass article by the pontil or punty rod. The hot glass object is attached at the base to the pontil rod so the glass blower can more easily handle it during the final shaping and finishing. When snapped off the pontil, a round scar remains which, on finer quality pieces, is polished smooth.

PONTIL ROD or PUNTY ROD - Metal rod that the glassmaker attaches to the bottom of an article to facilitate handling of the hot glass.

RIGAREE - Applied ribbon-like crimped decoration which highlights some types of Victorian Art glass. It is a form of APPLIQUÉD decoration.

SANDCASTING - A technique of ladling hot glass into a cast made of sand, with forms and details impressed into the sand by a positive model.

SATIN - A finishing technique where the surface of an item is exposed to hydrofluoric acid to produce a smooth, velvet-like texture. (See ACID FINISH)

SHOP - Glass industry term for a crew of people that works together to produce handmade glass items.

SICKNESS - A term referring to cloudy staining found in glass items, especially bottles, decanters and vases. Sickness occurs when a liquid is allowed to stand in a piece for a long period of time causing a chemical deterioration of the interior surface. Some sickness can be "cured" by thorough cleaning, though in worse cases, only re-polishing the surface will restore the luster.

SPALL - A shallow rounded flake on a glass object, generally near the rim of a piece.

SPATTER - A spotted or multi-colored glass usually having a white inner casing and a clear outer casing. Like OVERSHOT glass, SPATTER is produced by rolling the gather in minute glass particles; but SPATTER is then cased to produce a smooth surface where OVERSHOT glass is uneven or rough to the touch.

TEARDROP - A DELIBERATELY PLACED INCLUSION IN A PIECE OF GLASS, FORMED BY A BUBBLE OF AIR. THEY ARE OFTEN USED TO HIGHLIGHT THE STOPPER OF A DECANTER OR IN THE STEMS OF GOBLETS, AND OTHER STEMWARE.

TURN - GLASS INDUSTRY TERM FOR THE SHIFT WORKED BY A SHOP (GLASS CREW). A TURN IS MEASURED BY A QUOTA OF GLASS IT WAS EXPECTED TO PRODUCE, NOT BY A SET AMOUNT OF TIME. (E.G. 300 PIECES RATHER THAN 8 HOURS PER TURN.)

VETRO A FILI - TECHNIQUE OF THREADING OPAQUE OR COLORED GLASS WITHIN CLEAR GLASS.

VETRO A RETORTI - A MORE COMPLICATED FORM OF **FILIGREE** GLASS WITH THREADS OF OPAQUE AND COLORLESS GLASS TWISTED AND PULLED INTO **CANES**. THE **CANES** ARE THEN ARRANGED IN PARALLEL ROWS ON A PLATE, HEATED, FUSED, AND PICKED UP BY A CYLINDRICAL GLASS BUBBLE. THEY ARE THEN BLOWN INTO AN OBJECT.

COLLECTING GLASS

There are as many different ways to collect glass, as there are glass collectors. Some people collect by color, others by pattern, still others by company or period. Some have very refined collections that only include specific articles – like covered dishes or whimsies – while others collect single cup and saucer sets. Then of course, there are collectors who buy everything they see because they love it all and can't decide. Remember: there are no rules in assembling a collection. Buy what you like and enjoy your glass.

The following is a list of the more common categories of glass. It is by no means complete, but is meant to highlight some of the more popular types of glass and styles of glass collecting. As you read through it, you may discover that your budding collection has already fallen into a specific genre. For many collectors, the thrill of identifying something they just purchased rivals that of the hunt.

ART GLASS - HANDMADE GLASS THAT WAS PRODUCED FROM THE LATE 1800S TO PRESENT. THIS TYPE OF GLASS WAS HAND WORKED, SO NO TWO PIECES WILL BE EXACTLY THE SAME. TIFFANY, STEUBEN, LOETZ, LALIQUE, VENINI, ORREFORS AND DURAND ARE JUST A FEW OF THE COMPANIES WHO PRODUCED ART GLASS.

CARNIVAL GLASS - PRESSED GLASS THAT HAS BEEN TREATED WITH METALLIC SALTS AND THEN RE-FIRED TO GIVE THE GLASS AN IRIDESCENT FINISH. IT WAS USED AS PRIZES AT CARNIVALS AND COUNTRY FAIRS, HENCE THE NAME CARNIVAL GLASS. *VINTAGE* CARNIVAL GLASS WAS PRODUCED FROM 1905 TO 1920 AND WAS SOMETIMES CALLED "POOR MAN'S TIFFANY" AS IT HAD BEAUTIFUL IRIDESCENCE REMINISCENT OF TIFFANY ART GLASS BUT WAS AFFORDABLE TO EVERYONE. IN THE 1960S, SOME CARNIVAL WAS REPRODUCED IN NEW COLORS WITH MARKS TO DIFFERENTIATE OLD FROM NEW: THIS *CONTEMPORARY* CARNIVAL IS ALSO COLLECTIBLE TODAY.

COLLECTIBLE 40S 50S 60S GLASS - A continuation of Depression glass. This category includes patterns made by the depression era companies after 1940 and through the 1960s. By that time, most of the original glass producers from the depression years were either out of business or absorbed into other companies. Again, it tends to be machine produced and was inexpensive, every day glassware.

CONTEMPORARY GLASS, 1970'S – PRESENT – A modern day continuation of the art glass category. Contemporary glass refers to handmade glass produced by studio artists beginning in the last part of the twentieth century. Chihuly, Lotton, Lundberg, and lesser-known individual artisans would fall into this category.

CRYSTAL - Refers to better quality stemware and decorative items made by companies such as Lenox, Baccarat, and Gorham during the twentieth century. Crystal usually has lead in the glass, giving it that wonderful ringing sound when tapped gently.

CUT GLASS/EAPG - Glass produced from the early 1800s through 1915. The glass is heavy and the patterns are cut into it by hand using various types of cutting wheels on a lathe. Early American Pattern Glass was produced from 1840 through 1915 as well. Like Cut glass, EAPG is heavy, but the pattern is molded into the glass rather than cut.

DEPRESSION GLASS - Machine produced glass made in America from the mid-1920s through the 1930s. It was inexpensive and came in a variety of colors: pink, red, green, amber, yellow, blue, cobalt, white and crystal. Depression glass was used as premiums with purchases of food products and soaps, as well as given out in movie theatres and gas stations.

ELEGANT DEPRESSION GLASS - The name for better quality handmade glassware that was produced during the depression years and through the 1950s. Unlike regular Depression glass, which was completely machine produced, Elegant glass was machine molded then finished by hand – etched, polished, reshaped and ground. Elegant glass was sold in better gift stores and department stores, and was made for longer periods of time.

FireKing - Made by the Anchor Hocking Company beginning about 1940 and through 1976. FireKing was glassware that was advertised as going from freezer to oven to table to refrigerator without breaking. It included a variety of kitchenware — from mixing bowls and roasting pans to dinnerware lines. Hocking made FireKing to compete with Corning's **Pyrex Glass**, (whose name literally means 'Fire King' in Latin) and which was also a line of glass kitchenware. Vintage Pyrex is also quite collectible today.

Glass by Color — One of the easiest collecting formulas in the glass world is to collect by color. The most commonly collected colors are black, cobalt, custard, forest green, jadeite, milk, pink, ruby, slag, and vaseline.

Glass by Companies — Many collectors focus on the glassware produced by a specific company. Some of the best known companies are Cambridge, Dugan, Durand, Fenton, Fostoria, Fry, Heisey, Higgins, Higbee, Imperial, Loetz, Morgantown, Moser, Murano, New Martinsville, Steuben, Tiffany, Tiffin, and Westmoreland.

Glass by Country — Another popular collecting trend is to focus on the glass from a specific country or geographic region. American, Bohemian, Czechoslovakian, European Decorative, and Venetian glass are just a few examples.

Glass Items — Glass animals, apothecary, Avon bottles, beads, bottles, buttons, candleholders, candy containers, cartoon/promotional glasses, cruets, fruit jars, ink wells, insulators, jewelry, lamps, marbles, ornaments, paperweights, perfume bottles, shoes, shot glasses, and toothpick holders are only a few of the thousands of glass items people look for.

Select Bibliography

Arwas, Victor, *The Art of Glass: Art Nouveau to Art Deco.* United Kingdom: Andreas Papadakis Publisher, 1996.

Barr, Sheldon, *Venetian Glass: Confections in Glass 1855–1914.* New York: Harry N. Abrams, 1998.

Ed. Barovier, Marion, *Tagliapietra: A Venetian Glass Maestro.* Dublin, Ireland: Links for Publishing Ltd, 1998.

Bröhan, Torston and Martin Eidelberg, *Glass of the Avant-Garde: From Vienna Secession to Bauhaus.* New York: Prestel, 2001.

Charleston, Robert J., *Masterpieces of Glass: A World History from the Corning Museum of Glass.* New York: Harry N. Abrams, Inc., 1990.

Couldrey, Vivienne, *The Art of Louis Comfort Tiffany.* New Jersey: Wellfleet Press, 1989.

Cousins, Mark, *20th Century Glass.* United Kingdom: Grange Books, 1989.

Dawes, Nicholas M., *Lalique Glass.* New York: Crown Publishers, Inc., 1986.

Douglas, Mary F., *Harvey K. Littleton: Reflections 1946–1994.* North Carolina: Mint Museum of Craft and Design, 1999.

Duncan, Alastair, *Louis Comfort Tiffany*. New York: Harry N. Abrams, Inc., 1992.

Frelinghuysen, Alice Cooney, *Louis Comfort Tiffany at the Metropolitan Museum*. New York: The Metropolitan Museum of Art, 1998.

Gardner, Paul Vickers, *Glass*. New York: Cooper–Hewitt Museum, 1979.

Herman, Lloyd E., *Clearly Art: Pilchuck's Glass Legacy*. Washington: Whatcom Museum of History and Art, 1992.

Kuspit, Donald, *Chihuly*. Seattle: Portland Press, 1997.

Museum of Modern Art, Venice, Italy, *A Story in Glass: Robert Willson*. Venice: Edizioni in Castello, 1984.

Oldknow, Tina and James Yood, *William Morris: Animal/Artifact*. New York: Abbeville Press Publishers, 2000.

INDEX

Page numbers in italics refer to photographs.